# COOKING THE SPANISH WAY

Lerner Publications Company
A division of Lerner Publishing Group
241 First Avenue North
Minneapolis, MN 55401 U.S.A.

Website address: www.lernerbooks.com


Library of Congress Cataloging-in-Publication Data

Christian, Rebecca.
    Cooking the Spanish way / by Rebecca Christian.—Rev. & expanded
        p.    cm. — (Easy menu ethnic cookbooks)
    Includes index.
    ISBN 0-8225-4122-X (lib. bdg. : alk. paper)
    1. Cookery, Spanish—Juvenile literature.  2. Spain—Social life and cus-
toms—Juvenile literature.  [1. Cookery, Spanish.  2. Spain—Social
life and customs.]  I. Title.  II. Series.
TX723.5.S7  C5  2002                                    00-012185
641.5646—dc21

Manufactured in the United States of America
1 2 3 4 5 6 – JR – 07 06 05 04 03 02

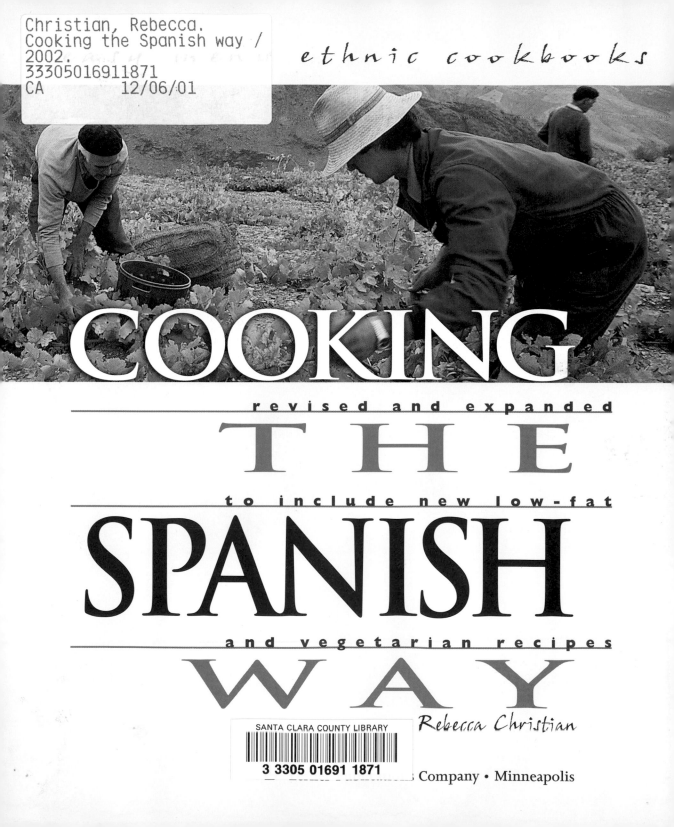

*ethnic cookbooks*

# COOKING

revised and expanded

# THE

to include new low-fat

# SPANISH

and vegetarian recipes

# WAY

*Rebecca Christian*

Company • Minneapolis

# Contents

## INTRODUCTION, 7

The Land and Its People, 8

Regional Cooking, 10

Holidays and Festivals, 14

A Spanish Market, 18

The Shepherd's Supper, 19

## BEFORE YOU BEGIN, 23

The Careful Cook, 24

Cooking Utensils, 25

Cooking Terms, 25

Special Ingredients, 26

Healthy and Low-Fat Cooking Tips, 28

Metric Conversions Chart, 29

## A SPANISH TABLE, 31

A Spanish Menu, 32

## BREAKFAST, 35

Coffee with Milk, 36

## DINNER, 39

Lentil Soup Madrid Style, 40

Salad, 43

Paella, 44

Stewed Vegetables, 46

Chicken with Rice, 48

Caramel Custard, 49

## SNACKS, 51

Fruit Punch, 52

Spanish Meatballs, 53

Cucumber, Tomato, and
Green Pepper, 54

## SUPPER, 57

Cold Fresh Vegetable Soup, 58

Spanish Omelette, 59

## HOLIDAY AND FESTIVAL FOOD, 61

Jijona Nougat, 62

Holy Week Doughnuts, 65

Ham Fritters, 66

Russian Salad, 69

## INDEX, 70

# Introduction

Spain brings to mind the sound of castanets, the feel of the hot sun, the spectacle of the bullfight, and the taste of hot, spicy food. You will find each of these things somewhere in Spain, but the large country is divided into many strongly contrasting areas. In some regions, it rains daily. In others, the climate is almost as dry as a desert. Styles of food from one region to another vary as dramatically as the climate. Whether it's succulent roast pork in Valencia, squid in the Basque country, or gazpacho soup in Andalusia, however, one characteristic is common to all good Spanish cooking. It uses the best, freshest ingredients. The country's history, land, and food have all contributed to the delicious varieties of cooking in Spain.

*Cold, fruit-filled sangría, or fruit punch (recipe on page 52), brings a refreshing taste of Spanish summer to your table.*

# The Land and Its People

Rising like a castle from the Atlantic Ocean and the Mediterranean Sea, square-shaped Spain dominates the Iberian Peninsula in southwestern Europe. After Russia, Ukraine, and France, it is the fourth largest country in Europe.

From the snowcapped mountains of the northeast to the scorched hills of the south, Spain is a land of geographical contrasts. Mountain ranges rise in northern Spain, and livestock graze in the mountain pastures. The ranges include the Cantabrian Mountains in the northwest and the Pyrenees Mountains in the northeast. Across the rugged Pyrenees lies France, Spain's northern neighbor. To the north of the Cantabrian Mountains stretches the Bay of Biscay, an arm of the Atlantic Ocean.

The remote Meseta region stretches across central Spain, covering about half the country. Farmers raise wheat and livestock on this ancient, high plateau. Off Spain's eastern and southern coasts lie the shimmering waters of the Mediterranean Sea. The sun-drenched Balearic Islands are popular Mediterranean vacation spots for many visitors each year. The Straight of Gibraltar separates Spain from North Africa to the south, and Portugal is Spain's western neighbor. Major rivers in Spain include the Ebro, which flows into the Mediterranean, and the Guadalquivir, which empties into the Atlantic Ocean along Spain's southwestern coast.

For centuries, Spain was known as "The Spains" because people of so many nationalities helped settle it. The country is still regarded as enchantingly different from the rest of Europe. Phoenicians, Celts, Greeks, Carthaginians, and Germans all left their mark on Spanish culture, but Romans and Moors (an Arab people) were particularly important. They developed irrigation systems to fertilize the once arid lands where fruits and vegetables have since been growing.

The Moors conquered much of Spain in the eighth century, and it took the Spaniards seven hundred years to drive them completely out. In 1492, the same year that the Moors were finally defeated, Christopher Columbus sailed to North America for Spain. Spain went on to explore and eventually claim part of the southwestern United States, Mexico, Central America, and much of both western South America and the West Indies. Explorers brought back tomatoes, potatoes, beans, corn, vanilla, chocolate, and eggplant, which provided new adventures in cooking at home.

By the 1800s, however, distant foreign wars, bloody civil wars, and economic troubles cost Spain most of its empire. It remained a poor nation until the mid-1900s. Since then, investors drawn by business opportunities and tourists lured by Spain's beauty have helped develop the country's economy. It has changed from an agricultural to an industrial nation.

## Regional Cooking

Spain is surrounded by water on three sides. So seafood, including tiny pink prawns and giant lobsters, is a mainstay of Spanish cooking. Fishers' catches are transported daily by truck, even to landlocked central areas. Beef is seldom served except in the northern pasturelands. Chicken, however, is important in the Spanish diet, as are fruits and vegetables. Olives, oranges, and grapes for wine are grown in large quantities.

*This market offers cooks a wide variety of fish and seafood, fresh from Spain's coastal waters.*

*Croplands, edged with bright poppies, blanket this Spanish landscape.*

Hills and streams separate Spain's forty-seven provinces, a fact which once forced Spaniards to stay close to home. Because of this isolation, the fiercely loyal people of each province developed their own cooking styles. Climate and available ingredients helped characterize these styles.

In the restaurants of Madrid, Spain's centrally located capital, diners can sample foods from all regions. Variations of hearty stews made with pork, vegetables, and chickpeas are cooked slowly in earthenware dishes over low heat. Stews originally became popular in Spain because they are easy to cook in one pot over primitive wood and charcoal stoves. The appeal of rich, strong stews lingers on even in times when most people can afford modern stoves.

The rural areas outside Madrid parch in summer and freeze in winter. Few trees offer protection from the elements. Roasting of game is quite common here. Hunters prize wild boar, quail, turkey, pheasant, and deer. Suckling pig and baby lamb are also favorites.

Sparsely populated Estremadura, bordered by Portugal on the west, is famous for its spicy *chorizo*. This red sausage is used throughout Spain. Thin, wild asparagus cooked in butter is another Estremadura speciality.

In hot, dry Andalusia, a sparkling, fruity wine punch called *sangría* quenches thirst. Andalusian peasants were the first to create ice-cold *gazpacho* soup. This refreshing blend of tomatoes, garlic, cucumbers,

*Workers at a Spanish vineyard use traditional methods to crush juicy green grapes to be made into wine.*

and green peppers has become a national favorite. Fish fried to a delicate crispness is another speciality of this southern region.

The east coast of Spain is often called the Land of Rice. Rice is used in many dishes, particularly in *paella*, a savory rice stew of chicken, seafood, and vegetables. In addition to rice paddies, fragrant orange groves are found in eastern Spain.

Summer in Catalonia, a region in northeastern Spain, also brings fresh fruit to Spanish plates: juicy peaches, apricots, pears, cherries, and grapes all make excellent summer desserts, as do the many varieties of sweet melons found there.

Catalonian-style food, which uses garlic liberally, is also popular in northeastern Spain and in France, across Catalonia's border. *Calamare*, or squid, is a favorite from the Mediterranean Sea, which is to Catalonia's east and south. It is served "in its own ink," a dark, pungent sauce. And seasonal foods enjoyed in Catalonia include the fall's wild wood mushrooms and the spring's fresh young vegetables.

In northeastern Spain, the ancient kingdoms of Aragon and Navarre are known for their sauces—ingredients such as tomato, onion, garlic, ham, and roasted fresh peppers are combined to make smooth and unforgettable accompaniments to many dishes.

In the Basque country to the west of Navarre, the proud people have a deserved reputation for being passionate about food. Family ties are very strong here, and gathering together in the dining room helps cement the bonds. Herbs are used skillfully, and fish from the Bay of Biscay provide the inspiration for *sopa de pescado*, a savory fish soup. Tables groan under the weight of fowl, fish, meat, and vegetables—sometimes all served in different courses at the same meal.

The cuisines of Asturias and Galicia in northwestern Spain resemble the cooking of Celtic Brittany and Normandy in France. To fend off the chill of the damp climate, people in these regions eat rich and nourishing stews. A popular stew called *fabada* is made from a local white bean called *faba*, simmered with pork or ham. Because

Galicia is Spain's most important fishing region, seafood stews are also eaten, often accompanied by spongy yellow cornbread. *Empanada* is another well-known dish of Galicia: a hearty meat or seafood pie that is usually served cold.

## Holidays and Festivals

If you're looking for a celebration, you'll find no shortage in Spain. It is said there is a celebration, or fiesta, somewhere in Spain every day of the year. Many of these are small and honor a village's patron saint (a saint believed to protect the city and its residents). Other celebrations are massive, with thousands of Spaniards and tourists lining the streets to participate in the noisy, joyous revelries. Many fiestas, however, also have a somber and serious side to them.

Most holidays in Spain are religious. As the majority of Spaniards are Roman Catholics, holidays usually focus on Catholic saints and other Catholic figures. Other fiestas, however, commemorate different harvests, important events in history, or the beginning or end of a season. Some celebrations last for a short time, and others last many days. Spanish celebrations usually include dancing, music, singing, and processions in the streets. In a typical procession, representations of major Catholic figures, such as statues of Jesus or the Virgin Mary, are carried through the streets. For major fiestas, decorated streets, fireworks, and bullfights are often part of the festivities.

Food and wine are an essential part of a celebration in Spain. Family and friends gather to cook and eat a wide variety of delicious dishes. Paella is almost always served at fiestas. Other traditional fiesta foods include turrón, a honey and almond nougat candy, and mazapán, sweets made of a paste of ground almonds and sugar.

One of the most important holidays across Spain is la Semana Santa, or Holy Week. This Easter week celebration begins on Palm Sunday and continues until Good Friday. Holy Week processions are solemn. Massive floats carry huge, elaborate figures of Jesus, the Virgin Mary, and the saints. Some floats show scenes from the story of Jesus' life. The floats, many of which are lit with candles, are carried on the shoulders of many men. It is considered an honor to help carry a float. Walking next to the carriers are hundreds of people holding long candles and wearing long robes and tall, pointed hoods. The procession is accompanied by drumrolls and people clanking chains on the pavement.

Though the Holy Week celebrations are impressive in virtually every Spanish city, those in the southern city of Seville are the most famous. People travel there from all over the world, lining the streets day and night to watch and participate.

The serious nature of Holy Week doesn't stop the Spaniards from enjoying holiday feasts. Some traditional dishes include *pure de cuaresma*—a soup made with white beans, potatoes, leeks, carrots, and onions—and *cordero pascual*, a main course of leg of lamb with gravy on the side. This dish is often served with potatoes or white beans.

Small village fiestas are an important time for the village's residents. One fiesta in Culera, Andalusia, celebrates the town's patron saint and the fishing season. During the fiesta, the village's fishers solemnly give thanks to their patron, la Virgen del Castillo. An image of the saint sits in a church on a hill overlooking the sea. As the fishers pay homage to her, they pray for good luck throughout the coming year. In small villages and big cities alike, no festival is complete without a feast. In Culera, people might serve a dish of rice and squid cooked with onions and tomatoes for a fiesta dinner. To top off the fiesta, people eat a sweet pastry with coffee for breakfast the next day.

Christmas is an important time throughout Spain. This religious holiday is a time for families to come together. Some families attend a midnight Mass and tour their neighborhoods singing Christmas carols. Food, of course, is a major part of the Christmas festivities. Christmas Eve supper is always a grand affair with soup, fish, ham, roast turkey or chicken, salad, fruits, and cheese. Leftovers from the night before are typically served for Christmas day lunch. Spaniards eat large amounts of turrón during this holiday.

Spanish children wait until January 6, el Día de los Reyes Magos—Three Kings' Day (also called Epiphany)—to open their presents. Many towns celebrate this holiday by throwing candy to children from floats during a procession. On January 5, children set their shoes out on porches and balconies. The next day, the children check their shoes to find what the three kings left during the night. People make a special sweet bread, called *rosca de reyes*, during this holiday. The bread contains nuts, fruits, raisins, and brandy and is baked in the shape of a ring. Traditionally, a small object, such as a bean or coin, is hidden inside. Whoever finds the object is supposed to have good luck all year.

New Year's Eve in Spain is a family celebration. At midnight, members of a family eat twelve grapes, one for each stroke of the clock, and drink champagne. People often do not go to bed until dawn. They usually retire after eating a breakfast of hot chocolate and *churros*, a type of Spanish doughnut.

Every year from March 12 to 19, the city of Valencia honors its patron saint, San José, and celebrates the end of winter. Locals celebrate this fiesta by building huge figures—often comical versions of historical and modern people—in the city's main squares. During this week, people feast, dance, and watch the first bullfights of the season. Prizes are awarded for the best paella, flower displays, and figure designs. On the final night of the fiesta, the figures are lit on fire. They burn long into the night as people celebrate in the city's squares.

Every summer, from July 6 to 14, a popular and hair-raising celebration takes place in the city of Pamplona. The fiesta of San Fermín, or the Running of the Bulls, marks the beginning of Pamplona's bullfighting season with a week's worth of action, wine, and spirited celebration. Before the festivities begin, people barricade the streets to create a corridor that leads to the town's bullring. Very early each morning, the bulls that are to fight in the ring that afternoon are released into the streets. Thrill-seeking Spaniards and

*One of the exciting highlights of Pamplona's fiesta of San Fermin is the fast and furious Running of the Bulls.*

tourists race ahead of the bulls. People have been wounded and even killed during this celebration.

A less dangerous part of the festivities in Pamplona is a race for children. An adult in costume, which includes a three-cornered hat, chases children around the streets in a humorous attempt to make them behave.

One fiesta in Alicante, a city in southeastern Spain, has food as its focus, but the food isn't eaten—it is thrown. At midday, trucks arrive full of tomatoes. For over an hour, the city's residents have an enormous tomato fight.

All over Spain, people celebrate carnival by enjoying a final wild fiesta before Lent. Lent is a time of fasting and reflection before

Easter. During carnival, regular daily activities stop, and people take to the streets, dancing, singing, and holding parades.

## A Spanish Market

Most people in Spain shop every day. Although the modern cities in Spain have supermarkets, shopping almost always is done at specialty shops. Dairy products come from the milk bar, meat from the butcher, and vegetables from the produce stand. Most towns of any size have a large open-air market with a roof, but no walls, to protect it from the blazing sun. Amidst rows of purple eggplant, red tomatoes, and bright green lettuce, merchants compete for

*Shoppers at Spanish markets choose from an array of fruit, vegetables, nuts, and other tasty items for the day's meals.*

shoppers' attention. Chickens and many kinds of fish are sold *al fresco*, or natural, with their feathers, scales, eyes, and tails. Some chickens are so natural, in fact, that they are still alive—clucking and scolding about their unhappy fate. Merchants kill them right at the market to prove to customers that the poultry is very fresh.

Every market also has several rows of bright pink shrimp, mussels in striped shells, and tunas so big that they are cut into slices as thick as steaks. Chefs prepare one type of fish, hake, by clamping its jaws onto its tail and frying it in a circle.

Olive oil is usually purchased daily at the market. This oil comes from the tasty green olives that are grown by the millions in southern Spain, and it is used throughout the country. Shoppers bring their own bottles to the market and fill them from an enormous container. There are almost as many kinds and qualities of olive oil as there are olives in Spain. Olive oil is used so often that many Spanish skillets never lose the smell of it, even when they are scrubbed clean.

## The Shepherd's Supper

More than half of modern Spain's people live in cities, and more Spaniards work in the manufacturing, construction, and mining industries than on farms. The standard of living in the cities has risen significantly, but rural life in Spain remains much the same as it did years ago. Farmers live in small towns or villages and travel to the fields in donkey carts. Also, because most of Spain's land is used for pasture, shepherds are often seen tending flocks of goats or sheep.

When I was in Spain, I met a shepherd and shared a simple meal with him. I had been exploring a castle in eastern Spain and was walking down a narrow trail toward home when I met a herd of baaing sheep. Their shepherd was having his dinner on a big, flat white stone—a picnic table made for him by nature. *"¡Hola señorita!"* he called to me.

Because the shepherd rarely talked to anyone during the day, some of the sheep looked up in surprise at the sound of his voice. As I looked at the sheep, it was hard for me to imagine that the woolly lambs would soon be the delicious meat served in northern Spain.

The shepherd was wearing a black beret, a small hat, that had not kept the sun and wind from his face. His friendly face was deeply tanned. He motioned me closer and offered to share his supper. In Spain, even strangers share food with each other.

The shepherd's supper was a small loaf of *pan*, or white bread, some chicken, a peach, an orange, cheese, and hearty red wine. It was not surprising that the shepherd was drinking wine with his

*A Spanish shepherd guides his flock along a dusty road.*

meal. Although in North America we often think of wine as something to drink for a special occasion, in Spain it is served with every meal except breakfast. Spain does have expensive wines, but red table wine is very inexpensive.

After finishing the chicken, which was prepared very simply, the Spanish shepherd offered me a ripe, fragrant peach. I accepted it with thanks and looked in my backpack for my pocketknife. In Spain, it is considered bad manners to bite into a whole piece of fruit. Instead, Spaniards peel and chop the fruit into bite-sized pieces before they eat it. Some Spaniards are so used to preparing fruit in this way that they peel it very rapidly in one continuous motion. Before the shepherd and I started eating, however, we walked over and dipped our fruit in the nearby stream. Fruits are served unwashed in Spain, and at most dinner tables a bowl of cold water is passed to rinse them in. Spanish people believe this practice makes the fruit taste fresher.

The shepherd, like most Spaniards, ate his cheese for dessert. Cheese sometimes appears as an appetizer or in the Spanish version of the sandwich, but it is usually saved for the end of a meal. Most Spanish cheeses are white and smooth. One exception is *bolla*, a robust orange cheese made from goat's milk.

After we finished eating, I thanked the shepherd and continued on my way. He raised his hand in farewell. Although his meal was a simple one, it was a delicious example of how good Spanish cooking can be. Many of the recipes in this book are simple, too, and only require certain special ingredients to give them the true flavor of Spain.

# Before You Begin

Cooking any dish, plain or fancy, is easier and more fun if you are familiar with the ingredients. Spanish cooking makes use of some ingredients that you may not know. Sometimes special cookware is used, too, although the recipes in this book can easily be prepared with ordinary utensils and pans.

Before you start cooking, carefully study the following "dictionary" of special utensils, terms, and ingredients. Then read through the recipe you want to try from beginning to end. Now you are ready to shop for ingredients and to organize the cookware you will need. Once you have assembled everything, you can begin to cook. Before you start, it is also very important to read "The Careful Cook" on page 24. Following these rules will make your cooking experience safe, fun, and easy.

*A rich caramel custard called flan (recipe on page 49) is a classic dessert, made from simple but wholesome ingredients.*

# The Careful Cook

Whenever you cook, there are certain safety rules you must always keep in mind. Even experienced cooks follow these rules when they are in the kitchen.

- Always wash your hands before handling food. Thoroughly wash all raw vegetables and fruits to remove dirt, chemicals, and insecticides. Wash uncooked poultry, fish, and meat under cold water.
- Use a cutting board when cutting up vegetables and fruits. Don't cut them up in your hand! And be sure to cut in a direction *away* from you and your fingers.
- Long hair or loose clothing can easily catch fire if brought near the burners of a stove. If you have long hair, tie it back before you start cooking.
- Turn all pot handles toward the back of the stove so that you will not catch your sleeves or jewelry on them. This is especially important when younger brothers and sisters are around. They could easily knock off a pot and get burned.
- Always use a pot holder to steady hot pots or to take pans out of the oven. Don't use a wet cloth on a hot pan because the steam it produces could burn you.
- Lift the lid of a steaming pot with the opening away from you so that you will not get burned.
- If you get burned, hold the burn under cold running water. Do not put grease or butter on it. Cold water helps to take the heat out, but grease or butter will only keep it in.
- If grease or cooking oil catches fire, throw baking soda or salt at the bottom of the flame to put it out. (Water will *not* put out a grease fire.) Call for help, and try to turn all the stove burners to "off."

# Cooking Utensils

*double boiler*—Cookware consisting of two saucepans fitting into each other so that any food placed in the upper pan can be cooked or heated by boiling water in the lower pan

*food mill*—A metal utensil with holes in it through which food is pressed

*paella pan*—A shallow, two-handled skillet used to make and serve paella, Spain's national dish. (Any large, oven-proof skillet can be used in place of this pan.)

*spatula*—A flat, thin utensil, usually metal, used to lift, toss, turn, or scoop up food

*whisk*—A small wire utensil used for beating food by hand

# Cooking Terms

*boil*—To heat a liquid over high heat until bubbles form and rise rapidly to the surface

*brown*—To cook food quickly in fat over high heat so that the surface turns an even brown

*garnish*—To decorate a dish with a small piece of food

*hard-boil*—To boil an egg in its shell until both the yolk and white are firm

*marinate*—To soak food in a liquid in order to add flavor and to tenderize it

*mince*—To chop food into very small pieces

*pinch*—A very small amount, usually what you can pick up between your thumb and forefinger

*preheat*—To allow an oven to warm up to a certain temperature before putting food in it

puree—To push food through a food mill or sieve or to whirl it in a blender or food processor to make a smooth, thick pulp called a puree

sauté—To fry quickly over high heat in oil or fat, stirring or turning the food to prevent burning

simmer—To cook over low heat in liquid kept just below its boiling point. Bubbles may occasionally rise to the surface.

whip—To beat cream or egg whites at high speed until light and fluffy in texture

## Special Ingredients

chorizo—A highly seasoned pork sausage

cinnamon—A spice, which is available ground and in sticks, from the bark of a tree in the laurel family

garlic—An herb whose distinctive flavor is used in many dishes. Fresh garlic can usually be found in the produce department of a supermarket. Each bulb can be broken up into several small sections called cloves. Most recipes use only one or two finely chopped cloves of this very strong herb. Before you chop up a clove of garlic, you will have to remove the brittle, papery covering that surrounds it.

garlic salt—Dehydrated garlic combined with table salt

lentils—The brown, flat, edible seeds of the lentil plant

nutmeg—A fragrant spice, either whole or ground, that is often used in desserts

olive oil—An oil made from pressed olives that is used in cooking and for dressing salads

oregano—The dried leaves, whole or powdered, of a rich and fragrant herb that is used as a seasoning in cooking

paprika—A red seasoning made from the ground dried pods of the capiscum pepper plant *pimento*—Small, sweet red chilies that come in cans or bottles and are often used to add color to food. The word is sometimes spelled in the Spanish way—*pimiento*.

*red wine vinegar*—A vinegar made with red wine that is often used with oil for dressing salads

*saffron*—A deep orange, aromatic spice made from purple-flowered crocus plants

*vanilla extract*—A liquid made from vanilla beans that is used to flavor food, especially desserts

# Healthy and Low-Fat Cooking Tips

Many modern cooks are concerned about preparing healthy, low-fat meals. Fortunately, there are simple ways to reduce the fat content of the recipes in this book. Throughout the book, you'll find specific suggestions for individual recipes—and don't worry, they'll still taste delicious!

Many recipes call for butter or oil to sauté vegetables or other ingredients. Reducing the amount of butter or oil you use lowers fat right away. Sprinkling a little salt on vegetables brings out their natural juices, so less oil or butter is needed. It's also a good idea to use a small, nonstick frying pan if you use less oil or butter than the recipe calls for.

Cutting meat out of a dish is another way to cut fat. But if you want to keep a source of protein in your dish, there are many low-fat options. Some cooks like to replace ground beef with ground turkey to lower fat. However, since this does change the flavor, you may need to experiment a little bit to decide if you like this substitution. Buying extra-lean ground beef is also an easy way to reduce fat. You could also try substituting meat with a vegetarian source of protein such as tofu (bean curd), tempeh (fermented soy beans), or seitan (textured vegetable protein). These meat substitutes are often sold in the frozen foods or health sections of supermarkets.

One way to make your desserts and sweet drinks healthier is to reduce their sugar content. Experiment by taking out more and more sugar each time you make the recipe. You'll be surprised to find out that desserts and drinks can still be delicious!

There are many ways to prepare meals that are good for you and still taste great. As you become a more experienced cook, try experimenting with recipes and substitutions to find the methods that work best for you.

# METRIC CONVERSIONS

Cooks in the United States measure both liquid and solid ingredients using standard containers based on the 8-ounce cup and the tablespoon. These measurements are based on volume, while the metric system of measurement is based on both weight (for solids) and volume (for liquids). To convert from U.S. fluid tablespoons, ounces, quarts, and so forth to metric liters is a straightforward conversion, using the chart below. However, since solids have different weights—one cup of rice does not weigh the same as one cup of grated cheese, for example—many cooks who use the metric system have kitchen scales to weigh different ingredients. The chart below will give you a good starting point for basic conversions to the metric system.

## MASS (weight)

| | |
|---|---|
| I ounce (oz.) | = 28.0 grams (g) |
| 8 ounces | = 227.0 grams |
| I pound (lb.) or 16 ounces | = 0.45 kilograms (kg) |
| 2.2 pounds | = 1.0 kilogram |

## LIQUID VOLUME

| | |
|---|---|
| I teaspoon (tsp.) | = 5.0 milliliters (ml) |
| I tablespoon (tbsp.) | = 15.0 milliliters |
| I fluid ounce (oz.) | = 30.0 milliliters |
| I cup (c.) | = 240 milliliters |
| I pint (pt.) | = 480 milliliters |
| I quart (qt.) | = 0.95 liters (l) |
| I gallon (gal.) | = 3.80 liters |

## LENGTH

| | |
|---|---|
| ¼ inch (in.) | = 0.6 centimeters (cm) |
| ½ inch | = 1.25 centimeters |
| I inch | = 2.5 centimeters |

## TEMPERATURE

| | |
|---|---|
| 212°F | = 100°C (boiling point of water) |
| 225°F | = 110°C |
| 250°F | = 120°C |
| 275°F | = 135°C |
| 300°F | = 150°C |
| 325°F | = 160°C |
| 350°F | = 180°C |
| 375°F | = 190°C |
| 400°F | = 200°C |

(To convert temperature in Fahrenheit to Celsius, subtract 32 and multiply by .56)

## PAN SIZES

| | |
|---|---|
| 8-inch cake pan | = 20 x 4-centimeter cake pan |
| 9-inch cake pan | = 23 x 3.5-centimeter cake pan |
| 11 x 7-inch baking pan | = 28 x 18-centimeter baking pan |
| 13 x 9-inch baking pan | = 32.5 x 23-centimeter baking pan |
| 9 x 5-inch loaf pan | = 23 x 13-centimeter loaf pan |
| 2-quart casserole | = 2-liter casserole |

# A Spanish Table

A Spanish table is often covered with a white linen tablecloth, and a vase of fresh flowers is placed in the middle. A pretty bowl or basket of colorful fruit, which grows so plentifully in Spain, can also give your table a Mediterranean look. Oranges, plums, lemons, peaches, or other fruit make attractive arrangements.

In Spain, the table is set with silverware, but the plates aren't added until it is time to eat. The food is dished up at the stove, one course at a time, and the plates are brought to the table after everyone is seated. With the exception of a paella pan, diners never see a serving dish.

*These cooks are hard at work preparing a delicious Spanish meal.*

# A Spanish Menu

Below is a simplified menu plan for typical Spanish evening meals. Two alternate dinner ideas are included.

## DINNER # 1

Salad

Paella

Caramel custard

SHOPPING LIST:

### Produce

½ head lettuce
2 lemons
2 carrots
2 medium-sized onions
1 sweet red or green pepper
10-oz. package frozen peas
1 head garlic

### Dairy/Egg/Meat

eggs
cheese (any kind)
milk
half-and-half
butter
bologna (optional)
12 small fresh clams or ½ c. canned clams
12 medium-sized fresh shrimp in shells or ½ c. canned cooked shrimp
6 oz. chorizo

### Canned/Bottled/Boxed

small can or bottle green olives
2 15-oz. cans chicken broth
white rice
vinegar
vanilla extract
olive oil

### Miscellaneous

salt
brown sugar
pepper
sugar
oregano
saffron

# DINNER #2

Lentil soup Madrid style

Cucumber, tomato, and green pepper

Chicken with rice

Stewed vegetables

SHOPPING LIST:

## Produce

3 onions
2 potatoes
4 small zucchini
1 green pepper
3 carrots
sliced fresh mushrooms
    or 1 3-oz. can sliced
    mushrooms
parsley
garlic

## Meat

2½ lb. whole chicken
    (cut into pieces)

## Canned/Bottled/Boxed

canned whole pimento
2 16-oz. cans tomatoes
1 8-oz. can tomatoes
2 15-oz. cans chicken broth
white rice
lentils
olive oil

## Miscellaneous

flour
pepper
salt
paprika
oregano
saffron

# Breakfast/El Desayuno

Breakfast for most Spaniards is a very small meal. Some Spaniards don't have much more than a piece of bread or a roll and *café con leche* (coffee with milk) until the middle of the day.

Once I shopped for my morning pastry in a town so small that the bakery, which was in a row of houses, had no sign in front. The baker used the back part of her house for the bakery, or *panadería*, and lived in the front. Since everyone in town knew her, there was no need for a sign. A villager pointed me in the right direction, and I found the bakery with my nose.

The bread is made fresh every day, brown and hard on the outside and soft and warm on the inside. A fresh roll hollowed out and filled with a few teaspoons of olive oil makes a between-meal treat for schoolchildren.

Because the bread is made without eggs and shortening, it becomes stale very quickly. But it tastes so good on the first day that it's made, it never lasts very long anyway. In fact, the butter and marmalade often served in restaurants and well-to-do homes are usually not even needed.

*A Spanish family enjoys a light breakfast of juice, coffee, and cereal.*

# Coffee with Milk / Café con Leche

*Café con leche is more milk than coffee and is very heavily sugared. Most adults drink it, as well as some children.*

4 c. milk*

4 tsp. regular or decaffeinated
   instant coffee

8 tsp. sugar

**1.** In a saucepan, bring milk to a boil over medium heat, stirring constantly.

**2.** When milk begins to boil, turn off heat. Add coffee and sugar and stir until dissolved.

**3.** Serve Spanish style in four clear, heatproof glasses.

*Preparation time: 10 minutes*
*Serves 4*

*To reduce fat, use
  skim milk.

*Café con leche is a sweet way to start the day.*

# Dinner / La Comida

Between the hours of 2:00 and 4:00 P.M. falls the *siesta*. Businesses close, schoolchildren are sent home, and working mothers and fathers rush back from offices and factories. At this time, the whole family eats a large meal of four to six courses.

The Spanish eat one course at a time. First comes the soup, then the salad, then the main course with potatoes, rice, or vegetables, and then the dessert. Adults often finish their meal with a cup of coffee, a glass of liqueur, or both beverages in the same cup.

After eating, many people rest. Although some say that fighting city traffic leaves very little time for napping, the custom remains strong in Spain. During siesta time, the usually noisy streets are silent.

*Paella's combination of rice, vegetables, and seafood has a distinctly Mediterranean flair. (Recipe on page 44.)*

# Lentil Soup Madrid Style/Sopa de Lentejas Madrileña

4 tbsp. olive oil

I large onion, chopped

I can whole pimento, drained and chopped

I green pepper, seeds cleaned out and chopped

2 tbsp. all-purpose flour

I 16-oz. can (about 2 c.) tomatoes, cut up with a spoon

3 carrots, peeled and chopped

2 c. lentils

I tbsp. salt

8 c. water

1. In a large kettle, heat the olive oil for 1 to 2 minutes. Add onion, pimento, and green pepper and cook on medium heat until soft.

2. Stir in flour. Then add tomatoes, carrots, lentils, salt, and water. Cover and simmer over very low heat for about 2 hours.

Preparation time: 30 minutes
Cooking time: 2½ hours
Serves 12

*This basic but hearty soup is a great dish to warm up with on a cool day.*

# Salad / Ensalada

½ head lettuce

1 hard-boiled egg, sliced

2 carrots, peeled and chopped

1 slice bologna*, cut into small
    pieces

1 slice cheese (any kind), cut into
    small pieces

12 green olives (optional)

2 tbsp. vinegar

2 tbsp. olive oil

pinch of salt

pinch of pepper

1. Wash lettuce and pat dry with paper towels. Tear lettuce into bite-sized pieces and divide it among 4 small plates. (The Spanish do not use salad bowls.)

2. Put egg, carrots, bologna, and cheese on top of lettuce. Top with olives, if desired.

3. Mix vinegar, olive oil, salt, and pepper in a bowl. Pour 1 tbsp. of mixture over each salad.

*Preparation time: 20 minutes*
*Serves 4*

*For a meatless salad, omit
the bologna.

*This simple salad makes the perfect accent to any meal and can easily be adapted to suit individual tastes.*

# Paella

*Paella has no English translation. Served in nearly every home and restaurant, it is Spain's national dish. Spanish cooks make it in a shallow, two-handled black skillet called a paella pan. The pan is taken directly from the stovetop to table, where the dish is served by the person at the head of the table.*

12 small fresh clams in shells or ½ c. canned cooked clams

12 medium-sized fresh shrimp in shells or ½ c. canned cooked shrimp

8 oz. chorizo or other garlic-seasoned sausage

2 tbsp. olive oil or cooking oil

1 2½-lb. chicken, cut into 8 serving pieces

2 15-oz. cans (about 4 c.) chicken broth

1 medium-sized onion, cut into wedges

1 sweet red or green pepper, cleaned out and cut into strips, or 1 whole canned pimento, drained and sliced

½ tsp. minced garlic

2 c. white rice, uncooked

½ tsp. oregano

¼ tsp. saffron

½ c. peas, fresh or frozen

1. For fresh clams: Cover clams in shells with salted water, using 3 tbsp. salt to 8 c. cold water. Let stand 15 minutes and rinse. Repeat soaking and rinsing twice. Set aside. *For fresh shrimp:* Remove shells from shrimp. Split each shrimp down the back with a small knife and pull out the black or white vein. Rinse shrimp and dry on paper towels. Set aside.

2. In a paella pan or large, ovenproof skillet, cook the sausage 10 minutes or until done. Drain, let cool, and slice. Set aside.

3. Heat oil in the skillet and brown chicken 15 minutes, turning occasionally. Remove chicken and set aside.

4. In a saucepan, heat chicken broth to a boil. Meanwhile, brown onion, pepper or pimento, and garlic in oil remaining in the skillet. Remove oven racks and preheat the oven to 400°F.

**5.** Add rice, boiling broth, oregano, and saffron to the skillet. Bring to a boil over high heat and then remove.

**6.** Arrange chicken, sausage, shrimp, and clams on top of rice. Scatter peas over all. Set the pan on the oven's lowest rack and bake uncovered for 25 to 30 minutes or until liquid has been absorbed by rice. *Never* stir paella after it goes into the oven.

**7.** Remove paella from the oven and cover with a kitchen towel. Let rest 5 minutes. Serve at the table directly from the pan.

*Preparation time: 1½ hours*
*Cooking time: 1 hour*
*Serves 6*

# Stewed Vegetables / Pisto Manchego

*Vegetable dishes in Spain are often served as a separate course and sometimes as a main course. Pisto manchego can be served in these ways and also as a side dish.*

¼ c. olive or other cooking oil

I medium-sized onion, sliced

4 small zucchini, sliced

3 medium-sized tomatoes, peeled*
    and chopped, or I 16-oz. can
    (about 2 c.) tomatoes, cut up
    with a spoon

2 or 3 potatoes, peeled and
    quartered

¼ c. finely chopped fresh parsley

I clove garlic, minced, or ½ tsp.
    garlic salt

1. Heat oil in a large heavy skillet or deep pot. Add onion and cook until soft.

2. Add zucchini, tomatoes, potatoes, parsley, and garlic. Cover and simmer over low heat until vegetables are tender (about 30 minutes). Pisto manchego may be served hot or cold.

Preparation time: 20 minutes
Cooking time: 30 minutes
Serves 6

*To peel a tomato, place it in a small saucepan
of boiling water for about 1 minute. Remove with a
slotted spoon and cool until the tomato is warm but no
longer hot. Use a small paring knife to peel off
the skin. It will come off easily.

*With its bright red tomatoes and green zucchini, pisto manchego is as attractive as it is appetizing!*

# Chicken with Rice/Arroz con Pollo

1½ 15-oz. cans (about 3 c.) chicken broth*

¼ tsp. saffron (optional)

1 2½-lb. chicken, cut into 8 serving pieces

4 tbsp. olive or other cooking oil

1 tsp. paprika

½ tsp. minced garlic

½ tsp. oregano

1 large onion, chopped

½ c. sliced fresh mushrooms or 1 3-oz. can sliced mushrooms, drained

1 c. finely chopped fresh tomatoes or 1 8-oz. can (1 c.) tomatoes, cut up finely with a spoon

1½ c. white rice, uncooked

½ tsp. salt

fresh ground pepper to taste

1. Bring chicken broth to a boil, sprinkle with saffron, and stir gently. Set aside.

2. Meanwhile, rinse chicken pieces in cool water and pat dry with paper towels. Coat chicken pieces with mixture of 1 tbsp. oil, paprika, garlic, and oregano. Heat remaining 3 tbsp. oil in a large skillet with a lid. Sauté chicken pieces until golden. Set chicken aside on a platter.

3. Sauté onion and mushrooms in the skillet until onion is almost soft. Stir in tomatoes. Add rice and toss until coated.

4. Add chicken broth, chicken pieces, salt, and pepper. Bring to a boil, lower heat, cover, and simmer until the chicken is tender and rice has absorbed liquid (20 to 30 minutes).

Preparation time: 1 hour
Serves 6

*To lower the fat content, try using fat-free canned chicken broth.

# Caramel Custard/*Flan*

You would have to look hard in Spain to find cakes, cookies, and other sweet desserts. Although pastries are occasionally passed around at the end of a special meal, sweets are generally saved for an evening snack. Flan is a common dessert that is sweet but just light enough to handle after a large meal.

## Custard ingredients:

2 c. milk

3 eggs, slightly beaten

¼ c. sugar

½ tsp. vanilla extract

## Sauce ingredients:*

3 egg yolks, beaten

¾ c. half-and-half

¾ tsp. salt

½ c. brown sugar

3 tbsp. butter

1½ tbsp. lemon juice

*For a simpler version of sauce, melt 10 caramels in a saucepan over medium heat. Add ¼ c. milk and stir constantly until completely blended (about 10 minutes).

1. Preheat the oven to 325°F. To make custard, warm milk in a saucepan over low to medium heat for 10 minutes, stirring constantly. Set aside.

2. In a large bowl, beat eggs, sugar, and vanilla with an eggbeater. Stir in warm milk.

3. Pour mixture into a 1-quart or 9 × 13 baking dish. Set the dish in a shallow pan of water and bake for 1 hour.

4. After custard has been baking for about 35 minutes, prepare sauce. Bring water in lower part of a double boiler to a boil. Place the first 4 sauce ingredients in the top of the double boiler. Stir and cook until mixture is thick and creamy.

5. Add butter and lemon juice a little at a time, stirring constantly.

6. Remove custard from the oven (custard is done when a knife inserted comes out clean) and pour sauce over the top. Flan may be served hot or cold.

Preparation time: 1½ hours
Serves 4

# Snacks / Tapas

Spanish cafés are wonderful places in which to sit and talk or just watch people go by. The purchase of a single beverage is a night's rent for a table in one of Spain's thousands of cafés. Many people spend an evening going from café to café, stopping to sample the *tapas*—bits of shrimp, egg, potato, and sausage—that are sold for a few *pesetas* a taste.

Albóndigas, *or Spanish meatballs (recipe on page 53), are just one of the many tasty items that might be enjoyed as tapas.*

# Fruit Punch/ Sangría

A common sight in Andalusia is people sitting at outdoor cafés sipping sangría. This refreshing punch is typically made from wine, brandy, and fruit juice, but the following recipe substitutes extra fruit juice for the wine and brandy.

Sangría is most attractive when served in a clear pitcher so that the floating orange and lemon slices can be seen. First drink the punch. Then dip into the bottom of your glass with a spoon to get the punch-soaked bits of fruit.

¼ c. sugar

1 c. orange juice

4 c. grape juice

½ lemon, sliced

½ orange, sliced

1 small apple or peach, cut into thin wedges

4 c. club soda

ice cubes

1. In a large pitcher, combine sugar, orange juice, and grape juice.

2. Add lemon, orange, and apple. Stir until sugar is dissolved.

3. Just before serving, add club soda.

4. Put ice cubes into 8 glasses. Pour sangría over ice and spoon some fruit into each glass.

Preparation time: 15 minutes
Serves 8

# Spanish Meatballs / Albóndigas

Meatballs in Spain are usually served as tapas, but they also make a delicious light meal, especially when served with a vegetable or a salad and bread. For a more substantial meal, soup may be added to the menu.

1 lb. ground beef*

4 oz. ground chorizo or other spicy sausage*

¾ tsp. salt

dash of nutmeg

1 tbsp. finely chopped fresh parsley

2 slices bread, soaked in water

1 egg

3 tbsp. olive oil

1. Combine meat, salt, nutmeg, and parsley in a large bowl.

2. Squeeze water from bread and add bread and egg to meat mixture. Form into about 36 small balls. In a frying pan, heat olive oil and sauté meatballs until thoroughly cooked and brown (about 20 minutes). Serve immediately.

*Prepration time: 50 minutes*
*Serves: 12 (as appetizers) or 6 (as main course)*

*Try substituting ground turkey and spicy turkey sausage for the beef and chorizo to lower the fat content of these meatballs.

# Cucumber, Tomato, and Green Pepper/
## Pepino, Tomate, y Pimiento

2 to 3 thin slices onion, chopped

I tbsp. finely chopped fresh parsley

½ tsp. salt

I c. olive oil

I large cucumber

2 medium-sized tomatoes

I large green pepper

⅓ c. vinegar

1. Combine onion, parsley, and salt in a jar with a lid. Add olive oil and let stand 30 minutes.

2. Meanwhile, peel and slice cucumber into at least 16 circles. Cut each tomato into 8 wedges. Cut green pepper in half and clean out. Slice each half from top to bottom, making 8 strips. Then cut each strip in half to make 16 pieces. Put vegetables in a bowl.

3. Add vinegar to olive oil mixture. Screw lid on jar tightly and shake. Then pour dressing over vegetables. Marinate vegetables for at least 30 minutes in refrigerator before serving.

4. Center pieces of cucumber, tomato, and green pepper on toothpicks and serve.

*Preparation time: 30 minutes*
*Marination time: 30 minutes*
*Serves 8*

*Vinegar and onion give this fresh dish a little extra kick.*

# Supper / La Cena

Spaniards usually eat supper very late in the evening. Around 10:30 or 11:00 P.M., a light supper, much like a North American lunch, is served. It is usually some combination of salad, fruit, cheese, sandwiches, and soup. This hour sounds late for supper, but remember that the Spanish rest in the afternoon.

*The versatile Spanish omelette (recipe on page 59) makes a good dish any time of the day.*

# Cold Fresh Vegetable Soup / Gazpacho

2 medium-sized cucumbers, peeled and chopped

5 medium-sized tomatoes, peeled and chopped

1 large onion, chopped

1 medium-sized green pepper, cleaned out and chopped

2 tsp. finely chopped garlic

4 c. French or Italian bread, trimmed of crusts and chopped

4 c. cold water

¼ c. red wine vinegar

4 tsp. salt

4 tsp. olive oil

1 tbsp. tomato paste

**1.** In a deep bowl, combine cucumber, tomato, onion, green pepper, garlic, and bread. Mix together thoroughly.

**2.** Stir in water, vinegar, and salt.

**3.** Puree mixture in a food mill or food processor, working with 2 c. at a time. (If you've never used a food mill before, have an experienced cook show you how. When entire mixture has been pureed, discard any pulp left in the mill.) Transfer puree to a large bowl and beat olive oil and tomato paste into puree with a whisk.

**4.** Cover the bowl tightly with foil or plastic wrap. Refrigerate for at least 2 hours. Stir soup lightly just before serving.

*Preparation time: 45 minutes*
*Refrigeration time: 2 hours*
*Serves 6 to 8*

# Spanish Omelette/ *Tortilla Española*

*A tortilla, or omelette, appears almost daily in a Spanish home. Spaniards eat the tortilla as a main dish at a light supper or as a side dish at the big midday meal. Slices of omelette can also be served as tapas. The omelette is good either hot or cold. Usually it is served hot and the leftovers are refrigerated for a snack. The nutlike flavor of the Spanish omelette comes from slowly cooking the potato and onion in olive oil. This unique taste is lost if any other kind of oil is used.*

¼ c. olive oil

1 large onion, minced

1 large potato, minced

¼ tsp. salt

5 large eggs, beaten

1 tbsp. olive oil

1. Heat olive oil in a frying pan over moderate heat. Add onion and potato and sprinkle with salt. Cook until soft, but not brown, stirring occasionally.

2. Add about ⅓ of the beaten egg. Using a spatula, lift up omelette at the edges and center to allow egg to run under potato and onion. Repeat this procedure until all egg has been added.

3. When egg is firm but still slightly moist (not runny) and golden on the bottom, run the spatula under omelette to loosen it from the pan. Then place a large plate over the top and flip omelette onto the plate. (You may want to have someone help you with this.)

4. Add another tablespoon olive oil to the pan and slide omelette back in, brown side up. Continue cooking omelette over moderate heat until golden on the other side.

*Preparation time: 30 mintues*
*Serves 2 to 4*

# Holiday and Festival Food

A Spanish celebration wouldn't be complete without food shared with friends and family. Holiday or festival foods can range from enormous feasts at the dinner table to festive snacks at a stand or at a café. The recipes in this chapter can be prepared for holidays or festivals, or year-round.

Tapas are also a festive food in Spain. You can find endless varieties of tapas at fiestas throughout the country.

*Los Gigantes, huge statues that parade and dance through the streets, are a popular part of the fiesta of San Fermin in Pamplona.*

# Jijona Nougat/ Turrón de Jijona

Turrón is a traditional Spanish Christmas Eve sweet made of nuts and honey. Most of Spain's turrón is made in hundreds of factories in the cities of Alicante and Jijona. The turrón that comes from these cities is often considered the best. The turrón from Alicante is made with almonds, while Jijona's turrón is made with almonds and hazelnuts.

rice paper or wax paper

I lb. blanched almonds*

I lb. hazelnuts*

5 egg whites

I c. honey

½ c. sugar

I tsp. cinnamon

*If you want a less nutty flavor, reduce nuts to 8 oz. of each kind.

1. Line the bottom and sides of a 9 × 13-inch cake tin with wax paper or rice paper. For thicker turrón, use a smaller cake tin.

2. Spread out the almonds and hazelnuts on separate cookie sheets. Put in oven and toast at 350°F for 10 minutes. Place the hazelnuts in a kitchen towel and rub them until the skins come off. Chop all nuts or grind in food processor until fine.

3. Whip the egg whites until they hold stiff peaks. Fold in nuts.

4. In a large pan, mix the honey and sugar and melt over medium heat.

5. Stir the nut mixture into the honey mixture. Cook over low heat, stirring constantly, for about 10 minutes. Remove from heat.

6. Spread the turrón into the prepared cake tin. When cold, sprinkle cinnamon on top. Then cut into squares.

Preparation time: 1 hour
Makes about 40 pieces

# Holy Week Doughnuts / *Rosquillas de la Semana Santa*

*These delicious doughnutlike treats are a common sight during la Semana Santa, or Holy Week. They are prepared mostly in the south of Spain, in the region of Andalusia.*

3 eggs, yolks separated from whites

¾ c. sugar

½ c. milk

peel from I lemon*

peel from I orange

I tsp. baking powder

3 c. flour

olive oil for frying

cinnamon, to taste

sugar, to taste

*\*Use a potato peeler or a zester to gently remove peel in small strips from the lemon and orange. Try to avoid getting the white pith, which has a bitter taste. Chop or mince the peel with a knife for even smaller pieces.*

1. In a large bowl, beat the egg yolks. Slowly add sugar, milk, and lemon and orange peels.

2. Beat the egg whites with an electric mixer until they form stiff peaks. Add to the egg yolk mixture. Mix carefully. Add baking powder and flour. Stir until mixture is soft. Cover and let rest for 1 hour.

3. Cover bottom of frying pan with 2½ inches oil. Heat.

4. Rub some flour on your hands and shape the batter into pancakelike patties (about 2 inches across). Fry in oil on low-medium heat. Flip doughnuts about 1 minute after they begin to float, when they are golden brown, about 2 minutes total.

5. Remove from oil, place on paper towels, and sprinkle with sugar and cinnamon.

*Preparation time: 40 minutes*
*(plus 1 hour for dough to rest)*
*Makes about 20 doughnuts*

# Ham Fritters/Buñuelitos de Jamón

*These tapas can be made with a variety of fillings. They are best when served warm and are small enough to be eaten in one mouthful. The batter can be prepared ahead of time.*

**Batter:**

½ c. flour

½ tsp. baking powder

¼ tsp. salt

1 large egg

½ c. water

1. Sift the flour, baking powder, and salt into a bowl.

2. Lightly beat egg. Make a well in the center of the flour mixture and pour in beaten egg. Mix.

3. Add water and stir. Batter should be a thin sauce but not runny.

**Filling:**

2 tbsp. olive oil

1 medium onion, finely chopped

1 c. diced ham*

2 tbsp. chopped parsley

2 cloves crushed garlic

pepper to taste

1. Heat 2 tbsp. of olive oil in a small frying pan and sauté onion until it is soft. Remove from pan.

2. Mix onion, ham, parsley, garlic, and pepper into batter.

3. Put enough olive oil in the frying pan to cover the bottom, about ½ inch deep. Heat oil over medium heat.

4. Drop the mixture by teaspoonfuls into the oil. Fry until the bottom of the fritters are browned. Turn them over and brown the other side.

5. Drain on paper towels and serve warm.

*For a vegetarian fritter, try substituting firm tofu for the ham. You can also experiment with flavored tofu.

*Preparation time: 45 minutes*
*Makes about 20 fritters*

# Russian Salad / *Ensalada Rusa*

This popular salad, which has little to do with Russia, can be found in most parts of Spain. It is often served along with other tapas.

1 lb. medium potatoes, peeled, diced, and boiled

½ c. peeled, diced, and cooked carrots

½ c. cooked green peas

½ c. cooked green beans, cut into pieces

salt and pepper, to taste

¾ c. mayonnaise*

1 clove garlic, minced

sweet red bell pepper strips, to garnish

1. Combine all the vegetables except the red bell pepper in a salad bowl. Season with salt and pepper to taste.

2. Mix the mayonnaise with the garlic. Gently but thoroughly fold it into the vegetable mixture with a rubber spatula. Garnish with pepper strips.

Preparation time: 45 minutes
Serves 8

*To lower the fat content of this recipe, try substituting ¼ c. of mayonnaise with ¼ c. of nonfat yogurt. If you like the taste, you could substitute even more of the yogurt for the mayonnaise.

This colorful, creamy salad is delicious on a summer day.

# Index

abbreviations, 29
albóndigas, 53
Alicante, 17
Andalusia, 7, 12, 15
Aragon, 13
arroz con pollo, 48
Asturias, 13

Basque country, 7, 13
bolla, 21
breakfast, 35
buñuelitos de jamón, 66

café con leche, 35–36
calamare, 13
Cantabrian Mountains, 9
caramel custard, 49
Catalonia, 13
chicken with rice, 48
chorizo, 12, 26
Christmas, 15–16
churros, 16
coffee with milk, 36
cooking safety, 24
cooking terms, 25–26
cooking utensils, 25
cordero pascual, 15

dinner recipes, 40–49

Ebro River, 9

empanada, 14
ensalada, 43
ensalada rusa, 69
Estremadura, 12

fabada, 13
flan, 49
fruit punch, 52

Galicia, 13
gazpacho, 12, 58
Guadalquivir River, 9

hake, 19
ham fritters, 66
healthy cooking, 28
holiday and festival food, 61–69
holidays and festivals, 14–18
Holy Week, 14–15
Holy Week doughnuts, 65

lentil soup Madrid style, 40
low-fat cooking tips, 28

Madrid, 11
mazapán, 14
Meseta, 9
metric conversions, 29

Navarre, 13

*paella,* 13, 31, 44—45
Pamplona, 16
*pan,* 20
*pepino, tomate, y pimiento,* 54
*pisto manchego,* 46
*pure de cuaresma,* 15
Pyrenees Mountains, 9

regional cooking, 7, 10—14
*rosca de reyes,* 16
*rosquillas de la semana santa,* 65
Running of the Bulls, 16—17
Russian salad, 69

safety rules, 24
salad, 43
*sangría,* 12, 52
*sopa de lentejas madrileña,* 40
Spain, 8—10, 11
Spanish dining table, 31
Spanish market, 18—19
Spanish meatballs, 53
Spanish menu, 32—33
Spanish omelette, 59
special ingredients, 26—27
stewed vegetables, 46
supper recipes, 58—59

*tapas,* 51, 61
Three Kings' Day, 16
*tortilla española,* 59

*turrón,* 14
*turrón de jijona,* 62

Valencia, 7, 16
vegetable soup, 58

# About the Author

Rebecca Christian acquired her taste for paella and other Spanish specialties while teaching English in Barcelona, Spain. Christian is a freelance writer based in Des Moines, Iowa. She has written several books and many magazines and newspaper articles, for which she has won a number of journalistic awards. A graduate of Iowa State University in Ames, she has also been a reporter for the Mason City (Iowa) *Globe-Gazette*, the public relations director for the State Library of Iowa, and an editor/writer at Rodale Press in Emmaus, Pennsylvania. In her spare time, Christian enjoys reading, camping, gardening, and cooking. She often prepares recipes from *Cooking the Spanish Way* for her husband and children.

**Photo Acknowledgments** The photographs in this book are reproduced courtesy of: © Tor Eigeland, pp. 2–3, 10, 11, 12, 18, 30; © Robert L. & Diane Wolfe, pp. 4 (both), 5 (left), 6, 22, 37, 38, 41, 42, 47, 50, 55, 56; © Walter & Louiseann Pietrowicz/September 8th Stock, pp. 5 (right), 63, 64, 67, 68; © Blaine Harrington III, pp. 17, 60; © Roma Hoff, p. 20; © Tom McCarthy/Unicorn Stock Photos, p. 34.

Cover Photos: © Robert L. & Diane Wolfe, front (both), spine; © Walter & Louiseann Pietrowicz/September 8th Stock, back.

The illustrations on pages 7, 23, 31, 35, 36, 39, 43, 46, 48, 49, 51, 53, 57, 61, 62, 65, 66, and 69, and the map on page 8 are by Tim Seeley.